# OVERCOMING
## NEGATIVE FEELINGS

---

## A WAY OUT
OF
POOR SELF-ESTEEM GUILT ANGER FEAR AND TIREDNESS

BY
VIJAYADEV YOGENDRA

**HILL OF CONTENT**
**Melbourne**

This edition published 1997
by Hill of Content Publishing Company Pty Ltd
86 Bourke Street, Melbourne 3000
Reprinted 1997

© Vijayedev Yogendra 1997

First edition published 1995
by Foundation Press, Taringa, QLD

Cover design: Deborah Snibson The Modern Art Production Group,
            Prahran, Victoria
Typeset by:   The Design Group, Warwick, Queensland
Printed by:   Australian Print Group, Maryborough, Victoria

National Library of Australia
Cataloguing-in-Publication data

    Yogendra, Vijayadev
    Overcoming negative feelings: a way out of poor self-esteem, guilt,
    anger, fear and tiredness.

    (New ed.).
    ISBN 0 85572 274 6.

    1. Self-esteem – Psychological aspects. 2. Self-help techniques.
    I. Title.

    158.1

Our community and the community of the world at large are suffering through guilt, poor self esteem, other negative emotions and lack of purpose in living. This publication was inspired by the many people I have seen who are reaching out for assistance. I humbly dedicate this book to those who are searching for a meaning in life.

*Vijayadev Yogendra*

# CONTENTS

# Foreword

by Dr Alec Dempster, Consultant Psychiatrist

FINDING happiness and overcoming stressful, unhappy, negative feelings is a huge challenge to many of us in our personal daily life. This book explains the problems and solutions in a very helpful way. Today, millions of people are eagerly seeking guidance toward more meaningful achievement, "success" and happiness. Individuals seek this result through careers, family life, hobbies and so on. Self-help literature abounds in bookstores, and business-men, entertainers, "gurus" or powerful personalities of various types are sensationally promoted in workshops and speaking tours. Many people find these approaches beneficial and are inspired to believe in themselves, to set positive goals, organize their lives, and go on to find greater riches and perhaps also greater happiness. Yet often these don't provide the solution. "Success" as popularly understood often comes at a hidden and high cost to yourself and to society, and without the promised happiness. Psychological professionals often are asked to help sort out the consequences afterwards.

In some important ways traditional advice differs from many contemporary attitudes about the way to happier living. "High-achievers" in longer established traditions of personal development (religious or non-religious) have also possessed very powerful personalities, but the traditional developmental path has emphasized morality and avoidance of excessive personal self-focus. Students were taught to provide assistance or guidance to others, without proselytizing. In Western culture today, Mother Theresa outstandingly epitomizes the spirituality of the traditional path. Dedicated to her Catholic religious tradition of service to mankind and God, and spiritual development, she remains personally unconcerned with fame or egocentric power. She helps others overcome despair and gives love and happiness.

This book has a positive and happy message and is sympathetic to individual predicaments. It explains how negative feelings arise from attitudes, ego problems, and sometimes our earlier life experiences, plus lack of a deeper more spiritual approach to life, and what we can do about this. It also is an important psychological and social statement that does not compromise with the truth or popular views. We are warned of likely more gloomy times ahead for contemporary human society globally and that we should think carefully of the future in order to respond appropriately and positively. It clearly states that the contemporary egoistic social framework, the "world-view" of today, within which individual "success" is understood and pursued, has a very dark side indeed – that is ignorance, mass perversion and mass unhappiness. Our modern "motivators" have given us the superficial, attractive "quick-fix", and rather little of the intensely sober, perspicacious advice that this book offers.

The guidance presented in this book is from genuine, traditional authority, following on from the author's father who continued a long-established, carefully guarded Indian tradition. Full appreciation of the wisdom herein, as with all important matters, requires more than a superficial reading, or a simplistic mind set. Considerable time, with repeated contemplation and application of the ideas is required to make the best of this book.

A direct, simple and safe approach to your deeper personal growth is vital. Few persons develop a mastery, leadership, and knowledge which can safely guide others toward a deep personal development. Consider a master musician who creates beautiful music from an instrument, making most complex performances look effortless, and belying the vast skill which is the basis of their artistry.

Similarly, mature personal development leads to an authority which is evident in the intuitive, uncomplicated personal style of this author. Simplicity, clarity and reliability are the hallmarks of authentic mastery of a domain and the author of this book, Shri Vijayadev Yogendra, has this.

Perhaps a little disconcertingly to the modern intellectual, the author writes in directive fashion, and does not offer the material as theoretical debate. The author's use of language and the development of concepts is both firmly grounded, subtle, and yet somewhat unfamiliar to the reader at first. It avoids the familiar styles of debate, dialectic, or chattiness common to serious non-fictional books. The serious reader is advised to suspend pre-judgement, or "premature closure of opinion", to adopt an open-minded attitude of inquiry and learning, and allow oneself time to maturely think through the issues.

Yet this is not a book merely to think upon but is essentially a series of practical recommendations for learning how to live better. In an unpretentious way we are offered advice with clarity and incisive practicality that goes clearly beyond the limits of contemporary psychological perspectives.

The psychology herein needs to be compared with current prevailing psychological thought. Western psychology today posits a spectrum of problems from everyday minor worries to "major mental disorders", the causes and expression of which results from a combination of factors: biological or organic disturbances, inherited behavioural traits, learned behaviours which may be either appropriate or maladaptive, and significant traumatic events with conscious or unconscious psychological repercussions. This is generally how the professional of today understands personal psychological problems.

To help the individual, contemporary psychology often seeks to improve "ego-strengths" and eliminate "ego-weaknesses", and generally a strong "ego" is considered a healthy fundamental of mind and personality. The "ego" is typically understood as an "integrating" or "processing" mechanism that mediates interactions and conflicts between inner unconscious desires, instincts, feelings and our learned values of right or wrong, and also our sensory perceptions of the world we live in. It operates continuously, and mostly unconsciously, to give us a realistic conception of the world around us, and of our own self. Through it we assess the reality of everything, e.g. appearance, personality, behaviour and likely consequences. Furthermore, a range of "ego defence mechanisms" gives us the ability to manage our thoughts, wishes or past memories, and are supposed to help us cope with psychological stresses or threats. Ego defence mechanisms can vary from primitive strategies such as denial, to mature sublimation or humour.

However according to this book there are other crucial factors in human psychology. It explains that our basic psychological struggle is with confusion, ignorance, hidden spiritual realities, the influence of mass psychology, and the play of life which we find hard to appreciate insightfully. Development of an "integrated", mature, individual personality is vital. Attitudes, values and psychological habits – anger, guilt, fear, impatience, excessive attachments, loss of faith in life, and lack of self-esteem, sexual difficulties, bio-energy disturbances, and "ego" are crucial obstacles that affect us all and must be addressed. Otherwise these all can contribute to major psychological or physical disorders. Furthermore for any helper in this field, their personal strength of character, faith and self-knowledge is centrally important.

Our author has a different understanding of the ego. Referring to the "ego", or "our little ego" etc, immediately from the opening chapter, and informed by knowledge gained from deep personal meditative experience and traditional teaching, overall the author advises that ego is a negative, though unavoidable factor in us.

The important point is that without deep personal development we cannot see past our ego, and our understanding of self and the world is thereby limited. Ideas, rather than full experimental appreciation of the facts dominate our insights: similar to knowing in theory what an apple tastes like but never actually having tasted one or two.

Developmental immaturity, not academic theory, limits psychological understanding, and so the limitations of ego reduce our insight, like ripples on a pond disrupting clear views of the bottom, interfering with our vision of the true nature of ourself and reality.

Respected Eastern and Western meditative traditions use the term ego (or its equivalent) to describe a pervasive, habitual pattern of our "mind-body-personality complex" whereby our consciousness is focused into a narrow sense of self-identity – described as "I-ness". Extensive self-preoccupation – an "I" preoccupied mentality underlies our desires for achievements, objects, possessions, or pride, or "success" of various types. The ego-based "I" enjoys and is misled via enchantment, pleasure, materialism, the outcome of the resultant psychological attachments is associated pain, fear, and ignorance, and exaggerated emotionalism. The more involved we are the less we see this reality. Thus our ego is a major barrier, greatly afflicting us all (with rare exceptions), and precluding a more attuned, sensitive, realistic, and meaningful experience of life. This is not just superficial egotism, nor is it a vital mechanism to be strengthened. Overcoming ego problems requires a serious search for inner knowledge and personal growth. At the same time this book acknowledges the significance of individuality and uniqueness. Overall it is not just proposing a simple "standard formula" for everyone, and thus this "traditional" psychology is actually quite profound.

Finally, for those who are not deeply familiar with this approach to personal development, nor the author's style of language and terminology it may be helpful to briefly consider this. Throughout this writing there are connotations hidden in the use of terminology and concepts which are possibly unexpected, not always made explicit, and may perhaps be missed by the reader.

The author describes every human being as made in the image of God, and endowed with something beautiful – that is having "innateness" – and having to find every opportunity of nurturing and expressing this, in order to blossom as a human being. It seems 'innateness' is a quality, and this word was chosen as the author's conceptual and verbal way of alerting us to a sense of the positive, deep, inborn nature, or spirit, in each one of us, which it seems is often hidden by our superficial ego-bound ignorance and self-image. Unfortunately, many people are unable to sense depth or meaning in their existence, or any associated positive sense of goodness, and feel a sense of suffering with confusion and sometimes despair.

"Inability to be oneself" similarly refers not just to superficial feelings of lack of confidence but to a deeper level of ability to move toward escaping from the constraints of our acquired persona or psychological facade, from our underlying ego limitations, and thereby to feel and live with more of a sense of freedom. "Holding back a part of ourself", in contrast to holding ourself back out of fear, describes an attitude of detachment and keeping an awareness of ourself.

"Inability to find love" is mentioned in the first chapter, and refers not merely to emotionally-driven ego involvement of two persons. The ability to find love extends to mean the ability to find and remain constantly within a more positive state of being in life which involves more trusting, compassionate, respectful, caring for oneself, others, and for the whole of creation. When the author talks of "giving", the full scope of giving can be implied – up to the potential for total, selfless commitment of all of one's being, life and capacity in service to others.

"Faith" is highlighted by the author as a fundamental factor in the process of personal development and personal 'success'. For many this has strong religious connotations, but it need not be so as virtually all of us live with some faith, whether we know it or not, or we would be paralyzed otherwise. We act and plan as if tomorrow will arrive for us, even though we can't prove 100% that it will. But mere intellectual belief or "blind stupidity of belief" does not comprise faith. Eric Fromm said faith is part of the quality of character of a person[1], and the author of this book has elsewhere defined faith as "the ability to believe in the unbelievable".

This is an important book, which is deceptively simple. You are offered direct, definite statements and advice about the nature of human psychology and problems. The challenging sincerity, intensity, and depth of wisdom being offered differs from most popular self-help titles, especially the insights into human needs, desire, greed, ego, and detachment, and the purpose of life. It is sensibly detached and realistic advice. For the thoughtful reader the commentary on contemporary society and the human condition is profound, and develops hand-in-hand with the essential core-relevant, down-to-earth, practical personal guidance. It is advising us to "think Big" by leaving our "little egos" and our negative feelings behind, and find greater Success, Love and Joy. Undoubtedly it is a rare treatise, by an author with unusual knowledge of human psychology. A similarly penetrating account will not be easily found elsewhere.

1 Ch 4 in: "The Art of Loving" Fromm F., Unwin Paperbacks London 1976.

# PART I

# CHAPTER ONE
# Introduction

CONTEMPORARY society is not allowing the individual to grow from within. It provides crutches and superficial props, and promotes a false belief that all is well. Rather than finding strength within oneself, we tend to depend on others giving us strength through approval and status. In our dependence, we remain at the mercy of the whims and wishes of those around us. We feel obliged to put on a mask and become what we are being told to be. We are led to believe that superficialities are important. We become distracted from recognising that there are more worthwhile objectives to be pursued, achieved, and made part of our lives.

But at times we sense there is more to life and make efforts to pursue this further. We feel frustrated and angry about our present state. We may experience a sense of helplessness, remorse, disillusionment or fear — all these negative feelings may eventually result in depression, an anxiety state or a combination of both. Time and again we attempt to overcome this state. We try to motivate ourselves, develop new attitudes, and resolve to overcome old habits. Or we attend a course, and pursue one technique or another.

When motivated, we are able to follow a routine for a few days or so, and feel like we are actually doing something to manage the anger, stress, anxiety, fear, low self-esteem, guilt, or whatever is our problem. Then, somehow, an old habit of thinking reasserts itself — from past associations or deeply ingrained attitudes — dislodging the motivation to improve. The positive efforts being made are disrupted. Unable to consciously control our destiny, or feeling controlled by an unknown force in ourself — which causes disruption and distraction — we tend to feel further disheartened and depressed.

After repeating this pattern many times, we may reach a point where we are ready to face issues more fundamentally. We then feel an urge to go beyond a superficial approach, a wish to come to grips with the core features and causes of our guilt, anxieties, negative self-image and low-self esteem.

Consistently pursuing this more committed line of thinking and behaviour, in a small way we may start to find conviction, belief in oneself, and strong determination. This is without tackling too many issues at once and not allowing the forces of negativism in us to overrun the positive. Then we glimpse life beyond our negativism. We start to experience what it is like to break this psychological barrier and associated restraining forces. This experience fosters confidence, further efforts and positive experiences. We can then entertain the feeling of really getting somewhere, and begin to believe that control over our own destiny is being achieved through precipitating and practising a more positive approach, and reducing the influence of past conditioning and negative factors.

It is generally unrecognised that the mental capacity we use to perceive, communicate, and function with, is less than one tenth of the total capacity of our mind. Further, the part of the mind that we use is largely restricted to the conscious mind. The other aspect of the mind, what modern psychology terms the "unconscious mind", is usually unavailable to us. But the unconscious mind is crucially important because it holds the key to our future development.

This book focuses on describing practical approaches that assist us to utilize more fully the capacity of the mind toward further progress, toward finding a deeper understanding and experience of life, contentment and happiness.

As detailed later, in accessing this greater capacity of mind we have to gradually become more aware of the present, to be less caught up in regretting the past and anticipating the future, and learn how to live totally in the present. The non-conscious aspect of our mind does play a dominating role in our lives — but only if we permit it to continue to do so. We can choose: either allow our past associations, conditioning and memories, or our fears, apprehensions and anticipations of the future to take away from our functioning, and our experience of the present; or we do not allow this to happen.

The more we become aware of the present, the more we begin to form a positive approach to life, a habit of living in the present that grows over time. We must try in our everyday living to stay focused in the present, limiting the dominance of unconscious fears. Eventually, even suddenly, we find we have access to the whole of the mind rather than a very small part of it. Then our guilts, fears and negativity dissolve, rather than simply being disguised behind a facade of competence. Life becomes more meaningful and enriched. We begin experiencing what it is like to live beyond negative feelings and a negative state of mind.

Growing as a person depends very much on a holistic process of developing both body and mind, not just one or the other. We have to understand personal growth as the growth of the "body-mind complex". It requires patience, perseverance, consistency and dedication. The process can also be viewed as progressively reducing the dominance in our lives of the narrowly-focused personal ego, and beginning to allow a deeper part of us — the more spiritual dimension — to flower and become stronger in our everyday living.

# CHAPTER 2
# Poor Self-Esteem

INDIVIDUALS tend to have doubts about themselves generated from early childhood experiences. These arise mostly because a parent or someone the child respects has made repeated critical comments. This becomes an unconscious memory which, as the individual grows older, is built on by adding new instances of failures and lack of achievement. Through this process a negative portrait of oneself is drawn which is then used to highlight, magnify and search out future faults and negative qualities. This poor self-image becomes a habit. It also functions like a filter through which we interpret all of our experiences. As such, it becomes self-perpetuating.

The constant feelings of guilt and wrong-doing, of letting others down, not measuring up and not fulfilling the expectations placed on us, deprive us of any self-esteem. We have been demolished and pressured to believe that we are second-rate individuals. This takes away confidence, not only in what we may not have achieved or done, but also in the good things we have actually done. The guilt also inhibits us in relation to anything we attempt in our lives thereafter. Lack of confidence permeates through every aspect of our lives and irritates us. We are prevented from achieving more and tend to settle into a routine pattern of life, participating in a minimal way so that we make fewer mistakes, feel less guilty and evoke fewer critical comments from others.

Often feeling we are lacking a quality of excellence, we admire someone we feel is superior or better equipped, whether by their conversation, appearance, or air of importance and then use them to measure our shortcomings. This "not good enough" syndrome gives rise to jealousy, envy and a lack of contentment. The poor self-image, the self-portrait built up from negative memories, drives the individual to become more immersed in sensualism, greed and distraction — in other words: the ego.

Strangely, this poor self-image also tends to make us project an aggressive attitude towards others. It is not uncommon that the moment someone opens their mouth to say something, we go into a suspicious attack mode, assuming they are going to criticize or hurt us. Another example is when we are driving and a person in another car tries to attract our attention. There is a tendency to assume that the other driver wants to be abusive rather than, in fact, inform us that we have not turned on our lights as it is now dark. After we react in this manner, and recognise that the other person intended no harm, we are left with a feeling of emptiness and negativity that reinforces our poor sense of self.

We have a persona, the protective facade we have created with the help of our "little ego". It makes us defensive and also inclines us to become either outspoken and rash, or withdrawn and aloof. We create a facade of competence, behind which hides a person who is shaky with every new move he or she has to undertake. Fear is created, leading us to be stressed and anxious: "when is somebody going to expect something of me?", "When is somebody going to make a demand on me that I cannot fulfil?", "When am I going to be humiliated again, or embarrassed?", "How many demands can I meet?" Reacting in this way, we miss out on knowing who we really are, knowing what we really want in life and doing the things that can give us peace of mind.

As a consequence of having gone through all this trauma, we cannot find love. Here when we speak of love, we are not referring to romantic love but rather to the capacity to endure, suffer, accept and care for another. This love is so accommodating and caring that it gives the recipient joy and peace of mind. Our problem is we find that we are incapable of giving, or we do it in a restricted way, within the framework of our limitations. Yet, somehow, we know that as human beings we have a capacity to love and to give, and we sometimes feel terrible because we are unable to show this capacity in our everyday actions. We fall back into the cycle of reinforcing our guilt and diminishing our self-esteem. Although there are many variations of this pattern, this is the basic sequence experienced by most individuals. Various approaches to breaking out of this sequence are described in Chapter Nine.

Non-conscious forces in us are difficult to control. The conscious understanding we have battles against our subconscious and unconscious forces which pull us in directions contrary to our conscious aspirations. The resulting conflicts have many ramifications with which individuals must attempt to grapple. Psychologists, psychiatrists and social workers are often trying to deal with these conflicts. Unfortunately, most of them are ill-equipped to assist people in addressing the basic issues of life, and end up giving only textbook advice and short-term solutions. Ultimately, unwittingly, these professionals often reinforce the narrow ego-dominated experience of life because they themselves have not experienced anything beyond this, of a spiritual nature. In very few cases are people helped in a more fundamental way that will lead to finding themselves and progressing further in life.

We have quite often heard "we become what we think". This is very true. Just thinking in a concentrated manner can make us do things we want to do, believe in the things we want to believe in, and gain that which we want. If you think you're going to be alright, then generally you will be alright. So also, if you think you're going to be sick, sickness will tend to result. It is interesting to observe how people can lock themselves into situations just by saying "I think".

This, therefore, is an important approach and one should use it in a creative instead of negative way. We find that we are mostly negative in our thoughts. In absolute terms, our negative qualities amount to no more than a very tiny part of our total being. Yet we neglect our positive qualities and focus only on the negatives. Like a hypnotist, by continually giving our-selves these suggestions, these negative suggestions, we reinforce our poor self-image and negativity.

Following earlier comments about the mind, it can also be seen that another capacity of the mind is the ability to imagine. The imagination is a powerful attri-bute. It projects a scenario, an attribute or image of ourselves that we tend to reinforce and make real in our thinking and daydreaming. The imagination is a neutral power that can be used positively to improve our lives, or negatively to reinforce a poor self-image, as the case may be.

This is also why the statements we make to our-selves, and the images we project, are powerful things which we must learn to use positively. It is therefore good to emphasize positive thoughts and imaginings that are personally meaningful. Contemplating and thinking on a theme, for example, "everything is going to be alright", progressively contributes to breaking down our doubts and insecurities over time.

# CHAPTER 3

# Guilt

G UILT is a feeling of dismay, of not knowing if we have acted rightly or wrongly. It is a feeling of having destroyed something or caused loss, suffering and disappointment. Even though we may have lived in such a way as to have been helpful to others and done the right thing, past associations tend to weigh us down and detract from any positive self-esteem. All of this adds to the feeling of guilt.

Guilt and low self-esteem are closely allied. As has been explained, low self-esteem is a poor opinion of oneself related to negative unconscious beliefs, doubts, or feelings — our guilts, inadequacies and our sense of living through an ego-driven facade. Guilt refers more specifically to our feelings and thoughts that we have committed some offence, done something sinful and wrong, that we have failed in our duty and that we may be liable to some penalty. We feel we are responsible for specific failings or mistakes.

As human beings we have expectations placed upon us by various institutions and strata of society, which we are mostly unable to fulfil. For example, there are the expectations of our cultural group, parents, teachers, and our peer group. Maybe at times we lacked the capacity, or did not comprehend, or the expectations of us were too high or inappropriate. This results in a deep-seated feeling that we failed to deliver, that we could not do what was expected of us.

The sense of being unable to live up to the expectations of others, and the feeling of guilt this generates, slowly develops into a habit. It often progresses further into a tendency to feel guilty about anything and everything that goes wrong, as if somehow it is linked with us. In extreme instances, a person may feel guilty just because the sun is covered with the clouds and they feel somehow responsible. Of course, this is extreme but it illustrates how the proneness to feeling guilty can over-generalize to include anything and everything. It is as if the person says "I feel guilty all the time because I have done the wrong thing by my parents, or teachers, or friends and associates". This constant internal conflict causes the person to lose a lot of energy, generating mental weakness and often fatigue. It becomes a habit of putting oneself down and also transforms into a belief of never being able to measure up to the demands of others.

Guilt is also generated when one is indecisive, or lacks awareness about what is involved in making a correct decision which is in one's best interests. Guilt can thus also be a product of confused thinking.

There is also a deeper aspect of guilt which stems from the sense each one of us has of belonging to something greater, whether you call it the universe, the world at large, life, or whatever: deep within there is a feeling that there is a greater force that we are indebted to, that we have an obligation to find, to know more about and to relate to. Moreover, there is a sense that this force also has an expectation of us. But we do not know the rules, the laws that govern these matters. So this deeper aspect may perhaps seem subtle and unclear for many of us, who have had no conscious experience or comprehension of such matters. Yet it is there, in all of us, hidden in the subconscious.

We do not have the knowledge to deal with various expectations, be they of the family, educational institutions, our peers, or of nature and God. We have not been educated to understand and respond appropriately to any of these factors. So, we have grown up in complete ignorance of how to counter or to balance the demands made upon us. In ourselves, we have created and accumulated the burden of not performing or succeeding and measuring up. Hence the burden we have developed is a strong and enduring feeling that we label with this word "guilt".

In almost every step in life there is a tremendous expectation placed on the individual to be successful, to become an achiever. This pressure to be successful and the associated need to prove oneself — which seems to have become so dominant in contemporary life — is one of the root causes of guilt.

Guilt is a crippling phenomenon that should not be allowed to take hold of any individual. It is being increasingly found that many psychosomatic health conditions and chronic diseases can be readily traced to the presence of poor self-esteem, anxiety and guilt. Asthma, diabetes, some chronic pain and even cancer can be linked with the effects of these negative emotional states. Everybody, particularly parents and educators, must make every effort to ensure that we do not perpetuate, encourage and precipitate guilt in our children, teenagers and all with whom we come in contact.

In today's society, there is a lack of training available for developing positive mental health and learning the approaches and attitudes, such as the practise of "detachment" (described in Chapter Nine), that lead to finding deeper contentment and meaning in life. Our psychologists and psychiatrists and other practitioners need to look beyond their current tendency to focus narrowly on symptoms removed from the person's total life context and particular growth needs: they need to look seriously at the total development of the person.

Individuals attempting to manage negative emotional states require training in self-reliance, in the capacity to believe in themselves and the ability to become more discerning in their involvements; i.e. spending more time on those activities conducive towards personal growth. This should be a component in our secondary and tertiary education so that the students graduating have the wherewithal to deal with the pressures of society, and more specifically, the pressures of materialism and technology.

Ultimately, to resolve some of the root causes of guilt, we will have to learn to reorient our relationship with materialism and technology. To do so we will have to learn to practice detachment: performing all necessary duties and meeting our commitments, while also holding back a part of ourselves — a part that can remain free, can enjoy life unencumbered, and can contemplate and experience a deeper meaning in life. Mortgaging one's soul to desires, possessions and seeking recognition is not an enjoyable way to live.

# CHAPTER 4
## Anger

ANGER is displayed by people who feel trapped or find themselves helpless and without any sense of a solution. We are afraid of the outcome of the situation because we perceive that it may result in further frustration, loss of hope or not getting what we want. We tend to feel resentful and have a poor self-image. Extreme anger is typically associated with tremendous inferiority complex.

Anger seems currently to be part and parcel of growing up. We see men, women and children who are constantly angry; at the drop of a hat they unleash this emotion, create misunderstandings, hurt others, perceive different meanings in situations and ultimately do great harm to themselves.

Anger is not part of a healthy life and it cannot become a contributive part of an individual's growth. It reflects poor self-control, poor self-worth, and a lack of dignity and understanding. The whole pattern of anger arises from accumulated experiences of inadequacy during childhood and from being subjected to ridicule or pressures. As a consequence, the individual tends to develop strong feelings of an inability to achieve, giving rise to frustration and welling up into anger.

The angry person is not fully self-aware and has not thought through the events to which they are reacting. It seems, suddenly, some subconscious part of the person releases various anticipations, images and thoughts which combine, release their impact and energy, and find expression in angry emotion. Within, the individual is saying "It's bad, it's bad, it's bad, I'm hurting, I'm hurting, I want to hurt, I want to hurt, I want to hurt others, I can't handle it". In a state of hopelessness and helplessness one psychologically, and often physically, hits out, in effect saying: "I want to tell you, and give a message to the world: I can't take it any more, I've had enough, I can't think this one through, I don't understand what is happening to me — all I know is that I'm not handling the situation. I have a deep fear, hatred and resentment. I have been badly done by, I am upset and therefore I am angry".

Past traumatic experiences, conditioning and mental associations, projected from the past to the present or future, duplicating the past scenarios, also triggers anger. This recreation of the past distorts our perception of the present, giving rise to a belief that nothing will or can change. This anger is a cry for help, an expression of helplessness: "it is going to go on and on, I have to suffer it and I don't want to". Alternatively, we may have been conditioned to see anger as a means to control or intimidate others, and of attempting to satisfy our needs and get what we want.

18

To overcome anger one must give oneself time to reflect before becoming angry, and give oneself space from others, rather than allowing the impulse to burst forth, to explode in an unthinking way. Taking time to cultivate this behaviour or habit enables one to feel on top of things. Having gained an upper hand on the emotions the mind can direct energies and emotions in a positive way.

Many of us have a tendency to almost obsessively ruminate over past hurt and get worked up to the point where we feel explosive. Just like milk heating for some time, upon boiling suddenly froths up, we also can wait with fire underneath us and suddenly, uncontrollably, we may burst out angrily. The recommended approach is to avoid reaching boiling point, by turning down the heat through developing positive attitudes, and positive distractions and involvements in other activities.

A traditional Indian story of a very angry snake roaming the forest near a village, illustrates this point. The villagers knew of the snake being angry and vicious, and avoided the forest for fear of being killed by the snake. A wise person passing through this village planned to go via the forest to the next village. The villagers begged of him not to enter the forest, describing the angry snake to him and what it would do. But this saintly person had his own understanding and knowledge, and could not be bothered with fear of a snake. He proceeded into the forest. As he walked he heard the rustling of leaves, looked back and saw the snake following, and before he could move again the snake bit his ankle. Yet nothing happened, he kept on walking. With increased anger the snake struck hard again, yet the saintly soul kept walking. The snake became even more vicious, so the saint picked it up and said "What's bothering you, why all this anger?".

A belief in India is that when an egoistic, angry person is confronted, somehow humility overcomes them. Knowing this was no ordinary man, the snake begged of him to be forgiven and asked for guidance. The holy man put the snake down saying simply "don't bite", and walked away. After some time the wise man returned through the forest, and, remembering the snake, searched and found it bruised and bleeding. Reviving it with Holy Water, he enquired "my friend, what has happened?". Viciously the snake replied "On your advice, I gave up biting, getting angry at people, and look — the villagers have stoned me!" The holy man smiled and said — "Oh my goodness, I forgot to give you the second part of the advice: hiss, but don't bite".

This simple traditional story illustrates a number of principles. Most significantly, it is used to illustrate that within our lives we can hiss, can make a show or act as if we are angry, but it doesn't mean we have to be truly angry. Quite often the same results will be achieved by allowing others to know, through our acting, that we are not happy or content, we've had enough and want to be left alone. In other words, our anger can be overcome by a calculated approach to conveying our feelings and thereby helping others understand who we are, what we want, how we want to be treated and what we are wanting to become.

We must start understanding that anger is devitalising and dehumanising. It takes away our dignity, ultimately leaving guilt, fear and poor self-esteem. We should not suppress anger, because this can generate, over time, various health problems. Instead, we should aim to allow our anger to be sublimated into love and care; it is like lava flowing out of a volcano which is channelled into brick moulds, where it is shaped and then used in building and creating something positive.

Anger needs to be channelled, while gradually the underlying habit is dissolved. We can prepare for anger by rehearsing and affirming our intention to sublimate the energy of anger. The energy of anger can most easily be channelled through the arms, hands and fingers — by focusing on an activity you enjoy, whether it is gardening, pottery, stroking the cat, writing a letter, etc. These and many other creative activities can vent and alleviate the internal pressure and churning generated by anger.

CHAPTER 5

# Fear

THE basic cause of fear is lack of knowledge or ignorance; fear relates to what is unknown. The unknown is a huge domain for many people. For example, there are very basic questions that, consciously or subconsciously, every human being wants to understand. Where we came from, who are we, and where do we ultimately go? These are some of the unknown factors that leave us with a tremendous amount of uncertainty, doubt and fear.

When we have experienced some suffering, the fear of the unknown will often be transformed into a fear of suffering. In other words, fear also arises because we do not want to suffer. Thus trauma, suffering, anticipation of pain, loss of face and ridicule, are all causative factors in fear.

Fear is a part of life. It may develop as a reaction to some trauma we have experienced as children. It may develop earlier, because everything that happens from the time of conception, when the foetus is formed, to the time of actual birth is able to be assimilated. For example, if our birth was difficult, there is a possibility of a related fear developing. The fear stays with us and manifests in many ways including the fear of death or loss of life. Our thinking and anticipations later magnify and extend our fears, causing us to lose trust in our sense of life and to become frightened, timid and anxious.

Various mental associations we tend to have are inherently pregnant with fear. If we want to be successful, or are ambitious and have strong desires, then the moment a want or desire is expressed, fear is created. The mind projects this fear forward in time anticipating a lack of fulfilment, and it tends to be magnified by the imagination which dredges over past associations and difficulties. Fear can thus arise in relation to an imagined lack of fulfilment and achievement. Fear eventually develops into stress, anxiety and a disposition to perceive things in terms of threats. It then prevents us from thinking and acting clearly.

We know, at some deeper level, we possess inner qualities, or "gifts", and that the practical expression of these makes us better people. They include a capacity for patience, persistence, contentment, acceptance and joy. We very seldom recognize or understand these qualities. We do not use these capabilities in a practical way to overcome difficulties we encounter. Instead, we give free reign to our imagination and habits of thinking, building up false projections and anticipations which become threatening and frightening.

We pass through life receiving extensive input from people: parents, teachers, peers and others — all of which has amalgamated and assimilated in our mind, and provides reference points or a basis for our life. If this basis is too restrictive, or carries particular negative patterns and ingrained fears, then it is possible to correct it, recast it and fine tune it. There is no reason why others should interfere in our self-development and upset our balance by creating fears or dominating our life. Others can contribute much to our growth, but they should not hold us to ransom, causing us to lose self-esteem and our personal approach to life.

Fear is sustained only when there is a lack of decisiveness, when we are uncertain in accepting the outcome of our actions. Fear is a real issue when we have not clarified what is important and unimportant in life, when other people's perceptions and opinions dominate our thinking, and when there is no control over desires and sensual needs.

The most important factor in managing fear is knowledge — experiencing and knowing things, and through these experiences understanding life and oneself. Using such knowledge one can reduce and eliminate fear and worry, and thereby gradually develop faith in ourself and life in general. This is important because faith is the ultimate antidote to fear. As will be described later, through the steady practice of techniques which quieten the mind, developing greater clarity and objectivity in relation to our situation, and cultivating certain attitudes, we can gain more understanding of ourself and allow faith to develop.

# CHAPTER 6
# Tiredness

WE NEED to recognize that our present life-style is taking a heavy toll on us. Each one experiences the demands, expectancies, emotionalism, egoism, and pressures of success and ambition. This impacts on the society as a whole and affects each one of us individually. Thus, one increasingly common symptom of this lifestyle is chronic tiredness.

We are slow to recognize the basis of our fatigue and tiredness. We seldom stop to think, but rather let the momentum of our lifestyle carry us blindly from one phase to the next. It is as if we are helpless, with no recourse to changing our destiny, obliged to follow the process in which we are caught up.

While we remain enslaved to the pressures and dynamics of our self-destructive lifestyle, we fall prey to an energy drain that is not replenished.

It is through experiencing repeatedly the negative factors in ourselves that ultimately culminates in what is broadly called "tiredness" — that is, a lack of strength and a lack of desire to get involved in any and all facets of life. We seem to burn up a massive amount of energy in order to sustain negative emotions and feelings, whether they be fear, guilt, anger, poor self-esteem, resentment, or other variations of these.

Negative moods need energy to sustain and support them. The ideas, anticipations and imaginings under-pinning them require energy to keep going.

It is important to realize that energy is used up in entertaining thoughts and dwelling excessively on events and issues. More energy is lost in entertaining negative thoughts than positive ones. If at all, positive thoughts act to "recharge our batteries", especially when they are thoughts of love, service or care for others. Habitual negative thinking drains the system and makes one feel tired.

It quite often happens that one has a long sleep at night yet in the morning, because of the stress caused by dreams and uncontrolled thinking, one wakes up feeling tired and exhausted, almost "wrung out".

To avoid this energy drain, thinking and emotions have to be constructively controlled. More specifi-cally, tiredness can be overcome through controlling the quality of one's thinking, maintaining an adequate diet and nutrition, learning to have stress-free sleep in which the mind switches off, and sufficient exer-cise and recreation.

The mind should be absorbed in some pleasant involvement for its own sake. You might, for exam-ple, sit down in a chair and think of a special place that you have been, bringing back the sense of the feeling of joy that you experienced, the relaxation you felt in that location, and recapturing the state of mind in a restful and relaxed manner. Otherwise, any activity in which the mind can become positively absorbed, and move away from the day to day preoccupations of one's life, is useful.

To make changes and overcome our lethargy, we must stop and assess our predicament and decide to take charge of our own lives. We can then proceed from each action to the next, fully aware of our personal and health needs, looking at the consequences that may emerge, deciding which steps to take, and thereby reducing the loss of our energy, vitality and immunity.

It is not uncommon to observe people feeling tired just because they are bored; they have nothing to do and cannot engage their mind in a creative way. They lose initiative and enthusiasm for any activity, and this produces tiredness.

Tiredness has become a chronic and widespread problem. When people suffer various viral infections — Dengue Fever, Ross River Fever, etc. — their body-mind complexes are struggling to maintain an energy balance. Already taxed by the emotional factors alluded to above, they lose energy, sacrificing their vitality and immunity. All this amalgamates into a perpetual feeling of tiredness which is now recognized as "Chronic Fatigue Syndrome". Some of the practices described later in this book would definitely benefit people suffering this condition. This is particularly so for the person who is not yet caught up in the full-blown syndrome and is trying to gain some control over the symptoms of tiredness that he or she is suffering.

Our whole approach and habits of thinking have to change if we want to overcome tiredness and lethargy. A new lifestyle must be adopted which preserves our energy, safeguards our immunity and vitality, and leads to a healthier future. If we ignore the signs and do not carry out these changes, we will simply be allowing the process to take over, and will have to accept these consequences.

# PART II

# CHAPTER 7

# Our Current Situation

WHY do people find it so hard to love? Why has the word love become a stumbling block, much maligned, misunderstood, misused and disused? The question often arises as to whether we as human beings even have the capacity, the competence, the attitudes, the purposefulness of being to be able to love totally. Whether we as human beings can love and give totally.

Is it the fears or the anxieties, or is it lack of faith that is causing this inability to love unconditionally, selflessly? Could it be that we are too tied up in materialism and our minds are so preoccupied with the technological and industrial razzamatazz surrounding us that we are virtually "freaked out" and have lost our values? We seem to take our bearings more in the surrounding razzamatazz than in our own self, our own "innateness" and inner strength. Or is it selfishness and greed that has overpowered us so much that we are unable to think beyond this?

These are the questions that baffle anyone who is well-meaning and reflects on the scenario that is being played out by human beings. There is not one country in this world that is spared this phenomenon; there is not one race, one religious group that is

31

exempt. Among concerned groups there is now emerging a tribal mentality. This can distort the positive impulse that the group originated to express. This "groupism" is becoming more prominent. Many religious sects and organisations have become fanatical, particularly the fundamentalists who are trying to shake up the world through their own approaches.

But even among all these people who are well-meaning and positively inclined there is corruption and a lack of love. Lack of understanding denies them any real capacity to give and to care. Becoming narrow-minded, people cannot grasp any deeper meaning in what is happening.

One of the major causes of the negativity, the fears, doubts and lack of purposefulness may be linked with our educational systems. Currently education tends to be success-orientated; the curricula only cater to ambition. Excessive ambition and egoism gives rise to greed, selfishness, and a lack of love and the capacity to reach beyond our needs to others around us.

This may sound like an oversimplification but we must recognise that the most important things in life are simple. Our universities have fostered only intellectuals who seem unable to comprehend simple things. Consequently academics are very much tied up in prolonged terminologies, self-satisfied explanations and the presumption that they have the key to solve all problems.

It may not be exaggerating to add to this group the educationalists themselves, even the clergy, and other professionals such as doctors, psychologists, social workers, psychiatrists and those who are trying to explain away the present problems that humanity faces, without giving simple explanations, much less solutions. Our intellectuals and experts are hiding behind a facade, the "I know everything" syndrome.

Of course there are people in this world who are very caring, who are extremely concerned and who probably are confused as to how to rid our society and the world at large of this terrific problem of carelessness, confusion, thoughtlessness and callousness that we see around us. There are those who want a way out, but haven't got the guidance or practical strategies to improve their lives and become better people, and cumulatively let the society progress.

These comments are not intended to be damaging and hurtful. Nevertheless, it is the case that the majority of people, absorbed in their special fields, are not concerned and are insensitive. Other than paying lip-service, they have no definite intention toward finding any genuinely practical and helpful approaches to improve the lot of humanity.

It may seem oversimplified, but the basic issue is that we have to generate among men and women a much greater capacity of loving, giving, caring and tolerance. We have to address the build-up of guilts in many human beings. We have to do something about the poor self-esteem that people suffer from, that deludes them and stifles them. We have to do something about the tension and the stress caused by ambition and a narrow success-orientated lifestyle. We also have to do something about the expectations we place upon people, our children, our wives or husbands, and in the workplace. Ultimately we have to address our greed for material wealth and possessions. These are the fundamental issues. If they are resolved, then perhaps we will have started dismantling the present crisis and cultural degeneration.

The next ten years will be critical in the development of individuals. Without the faith to make sense of their own being and understand the plight of others, without a personal resolution to improve their lot and the lot of others, we may find ourselves in a society that will be mercenary and totally devoid of love and the feelings that make us realise the importance of life.

The prospect looms before us of a sterile society without values, a society without love, a society with an abundance of mechanical gadgets, robots and people without conscience. These people will do the bidding of those super-human beings who have amassed to themselves, through their egos, through their treacherous behaviour and thoughtlessness, the power that enables them to exploit those who are below them. The average person who desperately wants to be happy, who desperately wants to belong to a society of people who are kind-hearted and generous, who needs a basis from which to grow and become a fully-realised human being is going to be denied a future. For our children, the future will be even more bleak.

Every school, every school teacher, every school governing body, every school principal, must try and understand what is happening and how these events will lead to certain consequences of our actions. What is happening in many parts of the world, in scientific experiments and research, is that we dig up oceans and the earth, we release chemicals into the environment, we manipulate the genes of people and animals, and we bring out from laboratories various cures — most of which are ultimately unsuccessful, and all of which somehow further the degeneration in people, and the initiative to experience life more deeply.

If one sits down and correlates these various factors, the degree of resultant damage that has occurred over the past many years is startling. The damage is apparent when we consider the pollution, erosion, environmental changes, the numerous diseases, deficiencies and allergies, and the progressive weakening of the individual's immune system. All of this is creating in people a psychological decline. It is as if the brain has been affected and can no longer comprehend or think, and a gradual shutdown in the system of thinking takes place.

In our present age, there is an absence of those forces, ideas and understanding of life that have made great poets, writers, painters and musicians of the past. Contemporary artistic and creative works tend to reflect a base element of human nature, and not any deeper experience of life. It is a disfigurement, a projection of disfigurement on a mass scale that is occurring, in the various expressions of contemporary life. Can we honestly call this progress? Is this in any way significantly contributing to human beings loving and caring for each other?

We mostly now see people finding ways of escaping, hiding behind the various facades, and avoiding the basic issues of life. People seem unwilling to confront and face up to themselves and what is in front of them. This may sound pessimistic and critical but when viewed objectively this is what one sees. There is a lack of love and a lack of understanding of the simple things that will make life happier and more purposeful for all of us.

# CHAPTER 8
# Love and Relationships

M ANY individuals experience an inability to love and give beyond a narrow romantically oriented love. It is helpful to begin to recognise that true love is actually a gift — a free gift, unattached, unencumbered. This type of "unattached" love becomes a sharing, a way of life. Love is given without any strings attached. No matter how much you love, you actually never run out of love or lovingness. It creates relationships in which there is no tension, fear or anxiety. When constant, love does not hurt you.

When love becomes spasmodic, emotionally based, fluctuating and selfish, then it begins to hurt and cause suffering to others and oneself. A constant flow of reassurance is denied which may be needed, particularly by the emotionally insecure person. In loving another, what do you "love" in him or her? The body? This is true in most cases. Occasionally we love the intellect, and very rarely we love the spirit. Yet, in loving the spirit there is no question of possessiveness. This only comes when we love or identify with the body. It becomes a possession like any other material object and we love the object and not the spirit behind it. In the contemporary world, we rarely experience love beyond the romantic and sexual forms.

In every relationship there is an element of love. Love has a pivotal role in positive relationships. The powerful force and quality of love gives any relationship meaning and strength.

A person may be looking for friendship, a relationship, or perhaps acclaim and recognition. That person may go "all out", making all possible efforts, and yet fall short of other people's expectations. It is better to be what we are rather than what people want us to be. Try just being oneself. There is a great deal of anxiety in being and becoming what others expect. Living life according to others' expectations limits us and gives rise to feelings of failure. Friendships and relationships built on this anxiety are flawed. We should seek to use our God-given will to just be ourself: do not change unless it is for the better and one feels the need for it deeply.

How can a person, who doesn't know how, sing if people expect them to sing? Or a person who can't paint be expected to paint? He or she can't do it, but may be very good at carpentry, or surgery, or any number of other activities. It is better to seek out our own innateness, our own goodness, and our own strength in that goodness. It is better to focus our efforts on trying to express and display this in our everyday living.

Relationships depend on trust, care, consistency and love. No relationship can survive under the pressures of tension, moodiness, excessive expectations or selfish exploitation. In our present day society we see traumas and tantrums dominating many relationships. There is a degeneration that is exacting a cost, economically, emotionally and spiritually. This is largely because we are wedded to materialism, a success-oriented lifestyle, to greed and selfishness, and, significantly: egoism.

It is love that gives real meaning to all relationships: whether between men and women, between children and parents or between friends. And, above all between the individual and God. Love in a relationship is as essential as water is to a plant. It is the most fundamental ingredient in a growing relationship.

Very few people can live happily alone. The need for people, interaction with others, companionship and the need to belong, are integral elements of human nature. Therefore, it is imperative for us to learn how to cultivate proper relationships.

Relationships are essential to human survival, growth and continuity. The only thing that gives meaning to a good relationship is love. Love provides the nourishment, the substance and the will for that relationship to go further. Without love the relationship becomes sterile and impotent.

We must not forget the fact that relationships take time to grow and develop. They need to be nurtured with attitudes like patience, kindness, tolerance and acceptance. One has to invest effort into developing strong and lasting relationships.

People with poor self-esteem are afraid to go forward in life or are weighed down with guilt and have difficulties in developing good relationships. In seeking companionship, friendship and intimate relationships, we must cultivate our own growth; develop our "ownness" — our own sense of life and the expression of our unique qualities, and become strong in our effort to achieve a sense of balance and right attitudes.

By developing an element of consistent caring in our approach, we find in each individual there is an aspect that is lovable. This factor is the common denominator in all human beings and animals; and in everything material and non-material. This is the divinity or primary animating factor. This is what should be loved in the individual because it deepens and enriches our relationships, and promotes goodness and growth in ourself and others.

It is the duty of every human being to give that love to each other, to feel good about each other. This means that one has to educate oneself and understand the basis of one's impatience, anger, aggression, and unforgiving approaches. These are habits that have been accumulated while going through life: they are not habits of the spirit, but habits of the ego. One must learn to separate the habits of the ego from the habits that are inherent to one's more essential spiritual nature.

Love is a natural phenomenon; it spontaneously occurs when the ego is not involved in what we are doing. In every situation in life, we must find out how we can be more loving, more helpful and more caring — rather than be obstructed by the ego dictating to us and telling us why we should dislike, why we should be impatient, intolerant, angry, or why we should not love.

In a fundamental sense, the world is full of spirits manifesting as human beings with human egos. It is the egos which dominate our lives rather than the spirits. Collectively, we have to find a deeper sense of a shared purpose and acceptance of others. This will only be found on the level of the spirits, of our spiritual selves, in the conjoining of spirits, not of egos. The sooner we learn to overcome, to rehabilitate ourself and sublimate the ego, the sooner we will experience the capacity to love unconditionally and find peace in life. This is an inherent duty carried by every human being that we must seek to fulfil.

# PART III:
## PRACTICAL APPROACHES

# CHAPTER 9

# Approaches to Overcoming Poor Self-Esteem, Guilt, Fear and Anger

1. Change negative into positive thinking.

2. Replace irregularity with consistency.

3. Replace others' rules, standards, and expectations with your own — focus on being who you want to be.

4. Replace guilt with reasoned understanding.

5. Aim to develop as a beautiful person and contribute to others.

6. Decide to develop a practical focus on the present.

7. Reflect on refinement and growth versus dominance by the ego.

8. To find deeper peace and happiness, create new habits in thinking and acting.

9. Think deeply and earnestly, to reach a conviction about self-development, leading to growth.

10. Decide to gain control of your thinking, and thereby your life.

11. Understand and develop detachment for mental clarity and maturity.

12. Summary — Fundamental factors which lead to integrated personal development.

### 1. Change Negative into Positive Thinking

Negative thinking and feelings are reduced by consciously practising every day: catching oneself thinking negatively, minimizing the negative dialogue, and reminding oneself that one is working on bringing out one's positive qualities — or, as noted earlier, bringing in to our present experience more loving thoughts.

We adopt the attitude that we are now being honest with ourselves and no longer accumulating the stress and tension associated with maintaining a false facade. This relieves a great deal of pressure when we can feel that we are working on something over time, accepting where we are at present. We may experience doubts and fears over whether this approach will be successful, but try to persist and trust that it will result in definite changes.

Sometimes it is helpful to use devices that assist and prompt one to maintain one's effort to break down negative thinking. Writing a diary each day, practising identifying ones negative interpretations and thoughts about situations and people, and keeping a daily chart of these, helps begin to control stress levels and negative emotional states. In the diary, linking up negative thoughts with day to day changes in your mood and stress levels helps one to stand back and disentangle oneself from negative emotion.

One can note the circumstances and also try to identify what one was thinking at the time.

When we have learned to identify our negative thoughts about situations, we can then start to deliberately replace these negative thoughts with more appropriate and positive interpretations and statements. We may even list the most common negative themes that arise, and work out specific responses — more appropriate ways of interpreting and responding to situations. Contemporary psychologists have promoted these approaches as a component of what is now called "cognitive-behavioural" therapy. These techniques do have a useful role to play in learning to stand back and distance oneself from negative thinking patterns.

It is important to recognise that these approaches must not be practised mechanically or they will only yield superficial results; they must be *purposeful* to oneself. Sometimes one does not really believe the positive statements that one tries to repeat to oneself. It can take time and regular application until we can see and believe their effectiveness and their truth. Of course, these statements have to be realistic and meaningful to have impact in breaking down negative thinking habits.

One further example of this method of approach involves setting aside a brief time each evening to respond to a series of questions that seek to establish a habit of recognising and valuing the positive actions and thoughts which have transpired during the day. Thus, at the end of each day, write down ten positive or good actions performed, or personal qualities one has observed oneself exhibiting during the day. For example, (i) I was particularly kind today with my co-workers; (ii) I reacted well today when my boss criticised me; (iii) I was more disciplined than usual today with my eating habits; (iv) I managed to stop myself becoming overly self-critical and depressed today after I missed out on being selected at work to attend a training seminar. This procedure should be done regularly for three months, and can be resumed again at any time if the need arises.

## 2. Replace Irregularity with Consistency

Irregularity in habits can cause distress. Chopping and changing directions in life can also cause distress. Frequent changes like these should be avoided. One should aim to decide to focus on or become one thing, and stay with it rather than become everything that everybody wants you to become.

Doing or practising some specific activity in a regular and consistent manner over time is another technique that builds self-esteem and reduces negative emotions; it may be an exercise, a craft, a domestic task, or whatever activity preferred. Consistency tends to build a subconscious sense of achievement, a sense that one can do something, and this builds a foundation on which a robust sense of confidence and belief in oneself can be developed.

### 3. Replace Other's Rules, Standards, and Expectations with Your Own — Focus on Being Who You Want to Be

Poor self-esteem also results from the habit of assessing oneself by the rules of other people. Most persons have rules or standards for assessing themselves and others. We have to develop our own rules. Leave those of our mother or father, and anyone else, for them to follow. Recognising this, and reminding oneself of it from time to time can help to free us from the imposed rules we may often find ourselves conforming to.

Whatever the circumstances in one's life, it is better to be oneself or become what one prefers to be rather than what other people want one to be. So, just try being oneself. There is a great deal of anxiety in being and becoming what others expect one to be. Being oneself means that one stops struggling to create and maintain a certain image that is thought to be impressive to others, and acts more naturally.

### 4. Replace Guilt with Reasoned Understanding

To be free of guilt, start reasoning and thinking things through. Initially take small issues and understand them. It is helpful to discuss our perceptions with someone who is knowledgable and whom we respect. They can give us impartial, objective feed-back, which we can use to assist in dismantling the whole guilt mechanism that has been established within.

We should contemplate on the fact that no man or woman has any reason to feel guilty about anything under the sun. As human beings we are prone to make mistakes, and as human beings we are here to learn from our mistakes. So long as the learning process is going on, and so long as fewer and fewer mistakes are being made, we have no reason to be ashamed or embarrassed about anything.

There is not one human being born who has not made a mistake, who has not let down himself or herself, or fellow human beings. But this is not some-thing one should take so hard. It does not necessitate that one feel guilty, nor continue to feel guilt for a lifetime. Guilt is not an asset, and therefore should not be accumulated. People "fail" because it is meant to happen, to provide the opportunity for further experience and growth. Try to understand "failure" as an opportunity to learn, a stage in growth, and not a reason for guilt.

## 5. Aim to Develop as a Beautiful Person and Contribute to Others

Poor self-esteem comes from the negative image one has developed of oneself, and a belief in that negative image. Because one has been brainwashed into believing one is substandard, one believes and continues to feel the associated low self-esteem.

We must choose to make an attempt to clearly look at ourself, to objectively review our current situation. To do so, ask oneself the following questions: (i) What I have aspired to? (ii) What goals have I wanted to achieve in life? and (iii) How much have I actually done? Also, (iv) How have I contributed to others? And, (v) What can be my further aim in life?

We must recognize that we have made mistakes, but not to the extent that we have to punish ourselves. Every human being has been made in the image of God, and has come endowed with something beautiful. Every person does have this "innateness", and we have to find every opportunity of nurturing and expressing it. This is how we blossom as a human being.

We cannot let society at large stop us from growing. We must take nourishment from the soil of life, and blossom to our most beautiful state. And that should be the aim of our life: that before we die we want to blossom as a person, and contribute what we have to give, so that other people can enjoy us — like enjoying a garden and looking at the flowers.

A simple practical approach to assist in gradually breaking the cycle of negative feelings is to regularly pause, during the day, and try to recall the sense of love and care that one has received at different times in one's life, from childhood to the present. Experience how remembering and feeling this can give one joy and release fear and tension. Then attempt to prolong this feeling for a few minutes. Next, see if one can in turn think of someone close and project this feeling of love welling up within one towards them. Repeating this exercise regularly will enable one to experience more joy and less tension.

## 6. Decide to Develop a Practical Focus on the Present

Self-development does not result from following a few hastily gathered techniques, nor a few statements that we repeat to ourselves; nor an intellectual perception and approach. Self-development depends very much on a systematic practical approach where both the mind and body work together to achieve a meaningful result. One of the myths about self-development and personal growth is that it is something that is achievable through intellectual perceptions and psychological techniques for probing the unconscious.

An individual's self-growth comes from a decision not to go back into the past, and not to go into preoccupation with the future, but to do everything that is required in the present. We have to accept the present situation, be very clear about what is happening in the present, and very much work in the present in the things we do. Become alert to happenings in oneself and around one, and define and act on one's priorities and responsibilities, regarding the immediate day to day, hour to hour, even moment to moment situation, and don't disregard this by losing or preoccupying oneself in past or future issues.

## 7. Reflect on Refinement and Growth versus Dominance by the Ego

From a traditional Eastern perspective, the aim of overcoming the sense-bound ego was to give the individual freedom and knowledge of the Divine or the Universal Reality. The cycle of life and death, function and dysfunction, beginning and cessation, was understood as facilitating the development of a small being toward becoming a whole self.

In our lives, we are victims of two opposing principles: the mundane-material and the spiritual-divine, polarised as negative and positive forces. It is through managing and balancing these forces that we progress with sublimating and overcoming the selfish-ego to find the greater "I" free of complexes and negative thinking.

The human ego is the sense of "I-ness" that orients all of our experience. The ego is a crucial factor in all interpersonal relationships. Where the ego dominates the relationship will not be mutually enriching, because there is always an element of hurt, anger or resentment. The ego distorts communication between people, because it produces disappointment and anger in all parties involved through the underlying expression of an "I want" mentality. Often, however, the disappointment and anger may be subtle, and not immediately felt.

Those who are trying to achieve progress and growth have to grapple with their selfish-ego and the deep identification with the ego-focused experience of life. When the ego is understood as being limited and restricted to the mundane level of life, then one can afford to begin looking at the larger picture.

The outcome of our efforts in personal growth will depend on how the ego is nurtured: the more the ego is expressed, the less the progress. We need to understand how to overcome the negative aspects of the ego, and to see how it can be utilized in a constructive and creative way. Yet it is not possible to clearly understand the ego merely through the intellect, or by reading books, as maturity of experience and inner awareness are needed to understand ourself and others, and experience what the ego within us is really like.

If we ask "who is it that gets angry?", the answer is "I". "Why do 'I' get angry?" Because "I" am not

satisfied or "I" am hurt. If there is a genuine or objective problem provoking these negative feelings, one
can look for another way of dealing with the problem, other than an expression of anger or other negative emotions. But while angry one becomes limited
in whatever role one has taken on.

What then, more specifically, is the ego? Restated,
the human ego is the sense of "I-ness" that orients all
of our experience. It is the "I" factor. This is the factor
that motivates and co-ordinates the functioning and
activity of the five senses. It, and the senses, are
associated also particularly with generating the experience of desire.

The senses give rise to the emotions, through their
interplay with the surrounding social structure and
culture, and through positive and negative personal
relationships. The ego has its likes and dislikes, wants
and needs, and is associated with pleasure and pain,
which are psychological structures or experiences
that we gravitate toward, or avoid.

The ego is the force of the "I" that expresses likes
and dislikes. Because the "I" is expressed in the social
sphere, there is a reaction from other people, and
from society in general. This reaction is accepted or
rejected by the individual. In other words, the "I" can
sublimate its own approach, or energy, and accept or
cushion these external pressures on an individual's
emotional stability. However, the "I" by its nature, is

unstable and unpredictable. It tends to be positive or negative, depending on the pressure we allow ourselves to feel. The issue then is how to neutralize the negative impact of the ego in our life.

When we are offended the "I" is hurt, or rather, our perception which is of the "I". The "I" is a perception defined by the answers to such questions as: "What do I think of myself? How do I look at myself? Am I intelligent or unintelligent, strong or weak, stable or unstable?" Outside reactions provoke changes in our perceptions of ourselves, and all these amalgamate to create an impression of self.

We are familiar with the ego but we do not have any sense of the self behind the ego: the real "I". We need to understand this real self behind the perceived self. You are more than what you perceive. Your perceived self is often the result of conditioning, social definitions, and other people's perceptions which we internalize, and which obscure recognition of the true nature of the self. The real "I" or self is part of Life itself, not something separate, and it gives rise to the urge to grow and express goodwill which resides at the core of our individual being.

There is nothing wrong with accepting our own goodness. This establishes a connection with the spiritual self. Negating goodness takes us away from the true self, and covering up weaknesses only creates more problems.

We can use humility in unwinding the "I". We may thereby neutralize the ego by understanding it. If we don't see how the ego is working in us, we don't know what to clamp down on in ourself. We need to be able to see what we have done wrong, acknowledge it, and then move on — because we are still aiming to express goodness.

It is helpful to reflect on questions that help us distinguish between refinement and growth, on the one hand, and dominance by the ego and suffering on the other. Such questions include: (i) Who is it that gets angry? (ii) Why do I get angry? (iii) What is the ego? (iv) How does it operate in my life? (v) How can I neutralize the ego? (vi) How do I become non-reactive? (vii) Why do I think of myself so much? (viii) How do I view myself? (ix) How do I develop a belief in myself?

Bearing in mind the problem of ego, we need to understand the meaning of belief — how should I best believe in myself and develop a sense of "I can do things". This sense is a result of repeated actual experience of belief in myself, with associated achievements. We need to explore the link or overlap between doing things with particularly ego-driven motives, and doing them correctly and honestly without fear or reservations, and without any motives that seek to bolster the ego. Thus we must find ways of expressing our "own self", without as much ego emphasis. Try by beginning to think of issues simply. We don't need to copy or imitate anyone. Be oneself. We have our own God-given knowledge, understanding and style of expression.

Understand one's own freedom; one doesn't have less knowledge than anyone else, but one is browbeaten and afraid to get in touch with it. One feels one will make a mess of things and this produces disbelief in oneself. One doubts ones own motives. But when one finds love and simplicity, knowledge becomes accessible.

There is ultimately no joy to be found in one's own small ego, but there is immense joy available in finding the greater being in us — the true spirit of men and women.

## 8. To Find Deeper Peace and Happiness, Create New Habits in Thinking and Acting

Looking at ourselves we may conclude that while we are actively participating in life our ego is dominating, dictating, and directing our whole lifestyle. We do that which pleases the ego and don't do that which in some way may be hurtful to the ego. This, however, is a superficial approach. With this approach we have never thought deeply from the heart, and believed in what our heart tells us. We have believed more in the mind and the ego. We have been brought up to deal with life on an intellectual and ego-centred basis.

As mentioned earlier, conscious understanding battles against those subconscious and unconscious forces in us which pull us in different directions, and are difficult to control. Most professionals are ill-equipped intellectually and personally to address the basic issues, so they reinforce the ego-dominated experience of life, such that few people are helped fundamentally to progress in finding their true self.

There is currently no education or university training available that can assist us to go deep within ourself and find a meaning and sustenance for the spirit, and to live in a spiritual way. Of course, there are a number of religious traditions that are accessible but these are no longer attractive to, or inspiring for many people today. Therefore, the only way we know how to live is in the mundane and the material, the technological, the competitive and success-oriented world. We identify with it, adopt its aims, and think this modern life and its pursuits is the sum total of who I am, of what my aim is to become in life. So this generates within us all these complexes of guilt, fear, anxiety, and poor self-esteem.

Those of us who are seriously interested in finding something deeper in life, or even simply sufficient self-control, much reduced fear and stress, and perhaps no guilt at all, must make a decision. It is possible to have a fear-free and guilt-free lifestyle, but we will have to work for it and practise day in, and day out, the attitudes, thought patterns and actions that will consolidate and create new habits of living that can sustain both peace of mind and happiness for us.

### 9. Think Deeply and Earnestly, to Reach a Conviction About Self-Development, Leading to Growth

Often we find difficulty, even though the urge is there, in getting down to the nitty gritty of changing things for ourselves. The problem is that we have so many doubts lurking in the deeper layers of our mind. These doubts, fears and reservations paralyse and inhibit us from acting and changing ourselves.

Often an individual can live for years without ever feeling like saying: "I would like to get in touch with myself; I would like to know a bit more about myself; I want to find out about the things that are hidden below the perceptible, the conscious, that which is beneath at the unconscious and subconscious level."

Perhaps the reason the notion of "meditation" is becoming more and more popular is that people are realizing that in order to reach the inner pressures, the deeper layers of the mind, and clean out the unconscious, one has to shut out the external interferences or distractions. One can then go within oneself, and find the unresolved problems, and try and tackle them in a creative and constructive way.

This approach, whether we call it self-discovery or understanding oneself, has to come through a conviction that one in fact really wants to do it. Because one has experienced, observed life and suffering, one may want to know more about why this is all happening, who or what causes it, and how to overcome one's inhibitions, and hence be free of the dramas experienced every day.

The contemplative process unfolds and enables one to see the problems of life as they actually are, in a correct perspective, provided one is sincere and honest, and deeply wants to achieve it. It becomes an inner growth and development. It slowly generates a potential for attaining a more refined state of mind and arriving at firm convictions. It releases in a person the capacity to go further in life.

One element of moving towards this inner contemplative direction is what might be termed a deep and earnest thinking over of certain aspects of life; thinking carefully, meaningfully, consistently, and sincerely. We have a capacity for activating the more refined part of our mind which is able to purify and bring into alignment the lower sensory-directed mind. Potentially, this refinement can be used to stimulate a genuine intuitive capacity. Over time this process leads to a transformation within ourselves through which we become more sensitive and observant, we become more helpful and consistent, and we feel happier —

which are all experienced as natural and effortless good feelings. Something deep within us begins to flower.

Consistent inner thinking can create conviction, and unfold and generate an urge to overcome difficulties. It is good to experience this for oneself. Keep in mind some of the teachings of great masters and wise souls, and reflect on what they have said, look at what we are actually experiencing and relate it to their thinking. It is necessary this be done carefully and in a dispassionate way. One must then define for oneself whether one wants to live in an illusory world with all its suffering, traumas, pain and discomforts, or whether one wants to be free of this and live in a more peaceful world by shedding the shackles of the ego and our fears. This is the decision we face. We must recognise that only the ego has fear; the spirit is fearless.

### 10. Decide to Gain Control of Your Thinking, and Thereby Your Life

Only we, and we alone are the author of our life. Nobody can make us see what we don't want to see. We can decide what we want to see, what we want to believe, and how much we want to progress. Applying the various approaches described here, if we decide to, and persist at it, will enable us to succeed in taking control of our thoughts. Most of the time it is as if our thinking is not done by us: it has already been "done" for us, and we are executing it. But we can decide to think things out and gain control over our own thinking. We should not allow ourself to be influenced by people who want us to live by their expectations.

## 11. Understand and Develop Detachment for Clarity and Maturity

When we talk of detachment or, for that matter, patience or aggression, we are basically referring to our mental or psychological approach to life — i.e. how one responds in a given situation. If the individual responds by becoming emotionally involved, he or she is unable to look at the situation objectively and becomes engulfed by what is going on. Detachment is an attitude whereby one distances the given situation from oneself, becomes objective, and views the whole situation as if it were happening somewhere out there, at a distance, rather than here, almost inside oneself. The detached individual can look objectively at the whole gamut of issues, options, repercussions and results without becoming so involved as to lose perspective and become prejudiced by one's own viewpoint, and thus react from this narrow basis.

The person who is attached cannot think of anything else but his or her own reactions to that attachment. Having a selfish stake in the matter is associated with an unconscious assessment of the personal loss and gain, the satisfaction and dissatisfaction, and the pleasure and pain coming out of the situation. So the individual's sense of security, confidence, and his or her "ownness" or inner sense of self-identity, depends upon their level of personal involvement in a given situation. The more involved the person is, the less they enjoy inner personal security.

On the other hand, a self-reliant person, a self-sufficient person, a person with greater understanding and self-control, can afford the luxury of being detached, because he or she is independent of the outcome of that situation. This person is not relying on outcome, and is not looking at the situation as being positive or negative for themself personally. He or she looks at it and says: "Well, that's that, it has happened, now I have to accept it, reorganize myself, refocus myself and act in the best way under the circumstances, without succumbing to the burden of pain, helplessness, anger or any other pressure that may come out of the situation."

The detached person is involved in worldly matters and acquires possessions, but has not "sold out", and is not possessed by the things surrounding him or her. He or she is free, uninvolved, and able to use all of the gadgetry, tools, and possessions without possessive feelings or identifying with any of them —

i.e. not needing possessions as a vital part of personal image, status or identity. While these possessions are there, the detached person can enjoy them; when they are not there, the best is done with whatever is available.

Importantly, this can be extended to relationships, friendships, and all social involvements because what we have is *now* — this very moment: it is available to us, the past or future are not. And therefore what we have now we enjoy, and what doesn't belong to us in yesterday or tomorrow, we don't worry about.

People can quite often misunderstand this attitude of detachment and think the person is callous or irresponsible, or that they are heartless. In reality, the person who becomes attached and overly-involved cannot clearly see his or her way in remedying, helping, or overcoming a situation, because the total involvement of the mind in the attachment distorts clear perception. A person who is detached, objective, and experiences life as a witness, can do far more, is far more helpful when the time comes, because his or her faculties are free and not overburdened or preoccupied by what is occurring.

If we examine our own life we will see that when we become attached we are non-functional in the sense of not being able to contribute to the welfare of our fellow human beings because of our own self-interest and emotional involvement. Paradoxically, the detached person is able to contribute more because his or her actions arise from a deeper clarity of perception. A clear rational mind, as opposed to an emotionally dominated mind, is capable of contributing and helping much more. Detachment allows us to be clear-thinking, with the full involvement of our faculties, and doesn't allow us to lose our independence and self-control which otherwise could be submerged in attachment.

Unlike emotions, detachment does not create reactions, does not take anything away from us, and does not involve us in such a fashion that we become less loving and less caring. The kind of love often displayed between men and women, between parents and children, and between friends and associates, usually binds in an emotional tangle where self-interest enters and the personal ego dominates. Such love then becomes very great attachment. There is a greater amount of interdependency and there is a lot at stake. This kind of emotional love can only precipitate eventual feelings of distrust, hurt, anger, impatience, and intolerance because of the fears of loss or non-fulfilment that attachment has created. But there is no fear when an individual is committed wholly and totally in giving, helping, supporting and caring, and says: "I am part of life, I like my fellow human beings, I love my family, and everything in life". This person contributes positively and consistently to the welfare of others without looking for the outcome of their contribution, but instead, the good of the person being assisted and loved.

It is here that we must repeat our understanding of the central importance of attitudes like detachment in making a person contented and whole. Detachment removes the hassles, the over-concerns and the negativity that attachments bring: "Not being emotionally involved, I am objective; not being involved, I can see clearly and I know what is right. When I'm involved I cannot see clearly; I'm attached, I want the result patent to my thinking because in that lies an emotional expression I am seeking."

Detachment is living a wholesome life. In fact, the practice of detachment leads to progress in life, health and happiness. Detachment does not allow the mind to fragment but makes it integrated and total. This is why the practice of detachment is also recommended for emotionally disturbed, psychologically devitalised, or spiritually bereft individuals. Attitudes like detachment are helpful to people who want to be free, clear-thinking, who want to grow and develop themselves as more caring and loving people.

Importantly, we must recognise that it is one thing to have an inner feeling of "I am happy," but understanding and becoming fully aware of what we are feeling is quite a different thing: to be so aware and dispassionate as to sense, as an observer, what we are

experiencing and feeling. This awareness is significant because it allows us not just to be submerged or
overwhelmed in our emotionalism, but enables one
to sense ones state of being clearly, and see things as
they are. This is another way of describing the mental
approach of detachment.

One must start cultivating the attitude of standing
apart and looking at oneself and, (as my father, who
was a noted traditional teacher, said whilst educating
us), looking as if in a mirror, trying to see what we
look like, witnessing it, rather than becoming it. To
stand apart and watch oneself grow is the beginning
of our own growth. To discriminate and decipher, to
come to conclusions about our growth, about the
mistakes we make, about the good things we do: all
this gives us clarity and maturity, and also leads us to
understanding the "I" and gives us a sense of what is
not "I".

It is relevant to say here that an individual's total
association from birth has been with his egoism and
whatever his ego has envisaged. There never has
been a time for the individual to know the real self
and therefore, the effort of improvement fails because we talk of the improvement only of the lower
self and not the higher self.

If we can understand and become more aware that
there are factors beyond what we think of as me and
mine, and that they are available to us as a higher

state of consciousness; if we can tap into this higher state of being and renounce the lower self and become a part of the higher self, that is, become a witness rather than a victim, then we will discover that we can achieve significant change in a much shorter period.

We can quite often change the various superficial modalities of our life like health, well-being, academic achievement, personality and confidence. All of these can be improved but in reality they do not add much to our self-image unless simultaneously, we can also improve our more fundamental approach to life.

## 12. Summary — Fundamental Factors Which Lead to Integrated Personal Development

When we begin to seriously consider how to progress further in life, beyond the superficial approaches to our problems, we have to start focusing on issues that are of fundamental importance. We have to start with sincerity and conviction, and an abiding faith that we will achieve real growth and the development we are seeking. This gives us a basis to proceed in a more systematic way that will take us further.

Some comments made by my father, who was a traditional teacher, may be relevant here. He suggested that we must start questioning aggression in ourselves, and think deeply on what it is that aggression has helped us achieve in life.

He suggested wherever possible we should try to be honest. The approach of being straightforward is quite often far healthier than the complications that come about by trying to deviate from the reality and the truth of the matter.

Wherever possible, one should try to be generous, caring and helpful and avoid exploiting others, wittingly or unwittingly. The latter generates a residue of guilt, which may not be at the conscious level, but we unconsciously record it as a wrongdoing.

Often greed allows us to want more than we need. We must contain and restrain ourselves from being too greedy or too demanding of what doesn't belong to us.

One must be willing to accept, accommodate and adjust to external factors. We must cultivate this habit and make it a part of our own thinking so that at any given time we have the appropriate attitude, no matter what happens.

Quite often one does not know what motivates his or her reactions. To achieve any measure of personal growth, one has to examine one's own motives.

One aspect of learning to understand one's motives is to endeavour to see oneself as others see us, rather than believing that one is always right in what one sees of oneself.

Rarely has it been suggested and encouraged in us that we should make life into an art form. My father advised there is an art to living, learning, growing, realising and this is something which has not been attempted by us. Currently, the "good life" is equated with success, ambition, selfishness, etc.

Quite often I tell my children and others that they must always have a dignity about them and behave in a dignified way, not lowering their standards or compromising their values. This requires developing one's own code of conduct and recognition of fundamental values and ethical approaches on which one's life can be based. Whether the world at large is kind or sincere doesn't matter so long as one decides to create one's own code of conduct and act in conformity with one's own thinking rather than being overpowered by other peoples' thinking.

The following suggestions summarize the development of such an approach to finding ourselves and achieving what we want in life and show more clearly how the various fundamental factors interact toward an integrated development.

*(i) Try and understand and then believe in a force or a higher reality from which one can take strength and guidance.*

When we consider an overall approach to life, we know that unless we have in fact a relationship with some higher force or factor in which we believe, unless we develop a philosophical ideal where we accommodate the idea of a benevolent factor, we will find it difficult to progress in any meaningful way and the ego will remain dominant because we have done nothing to curtail it. If we can sublimate the ego, which is linked with the root cause of poor self-esteem, we have a better chance of developing our full potential, and finding ourselves, and everything that we want in life.

(ii) *Examine the problem of the ego or the "I-ness"* which always seems to dominate, in the light of what we have discussed. In reality the true "I" has no fear and that "I" is removed from what we perceive and what is happening around us. What is happening is occurring at the level of the lower mind and not the true self. It is happening away from us and not within us. If this could somehow be verified, that will be very helpful.

(iii) *Try to be present in the present.* Try to allow the present to be so clear that the mind doesn't get distracted by past associations and conditioning, or future anticipations and fear. To live in the present in this manner enables one to experience and relate to what is in the present as it actually is. Aim to be absorbed, to participate and be involved in what is at hand, rather than allowing one's imagination to fuel anxiety or worry about what has already happened or what might happen. Absorb one's mind in what is at hand until the mind no longer becomes distracted by other associations.

It is important that one cultivate an awareness: to become continuously aware in the present that as a person one wants to continue to grow and experience one's own integration, maturing into a person who is respected and loved by other human beings.

We must not become too attached, too involved or too threatened by any result coming out of our efforts. We must remain detached and simply focus on what we are presently doing day by day — and let any results come in their own time without looking for them. This is very much a basic step that we will have to consider if we are looking at our growth.

We have also to decide to separate the non-essential factors in daily life and become more involved with things that lead to permanent satisfaction. We need to be able to associate with a better way of thinking, a better way of living.

Quite often our mind wanders away into useless pursuits and we have to bring it back to the present, reminding ourselves that the only important thing is now, the present; not yesterday or tomorrow.

(iv) *We must not always want things to happen the way we want them to be, rather we should accept whatever has happened and not be disappointed, and yet try to make the best out of it.*

Whether we call this approach contentment or patient acceptance, it is still a mental approach one has to cultivate. One can turn around a whole situation and accept what has happened just by redefining it: that what has happened must have happened for the best, thereby showing a faith in the ultimate reality, the ultimate will of that force that guides our destiny.

This aspect of God's will, the will of the Absolute, and the acceptance of that will, has to be done with a conscious effort, believing that this force is a benevolent factor. It is a force in all our lives that has our good at heart. We can never discern or know this factor from the perspective of the ego. It seems unfathomable and has a program of its own. It precipitates results that are not always palatable to the ego.

Development is an integral process. For example, we can see how developing a capacity for detachment is closely related to tackling the problems of the ego, to achieving increased focus, awareness and present mindedness, and also to finding a positive approach to acceptance of life's circumstances.

We sometimes become disillusioned with our progress because we become mechanical and, because we are expecting results, we become frustrated. What we are aiming to achieve is basically common sense, but we are looking for some "lightning bolt" insight or special technique.

The most appropriate attitude towards what happens to us involves acceptance as a key factor. Without being willing to accept, adjust to, and accommodate the various happenings, the various precipitants that we encounter, we can become very disheartened and disillusioned, and feel negative about everything, including ourselves.

(v) *Psycho-physiological Techniques* that comprehensively address the needs of the mind-body complex should be practised regularly (see next chapter). In doing this, we are trying to become more aware of our body-mind complex. It is a recognition that we control both of them rather than them controlling us.

Initially we tend not to be as concentrated as we could be. The person who is trying to develop his or her self-esteem must try to gain that type of mental concentration which enables one to be in the present with whatever one is involved. There are a range of techniques which can assist in gradually quietening the mind and developing the type of effortless and "one-pointed" concentration that enables one to experience life more deeply. Some preparatory approaches are described in the next chapter.

(vi) *Develop an attitude of giving love without possessiveness, constant caring, helping and feeling good about others and the world.* This love will flow more spontaneously as we sublimate anger, impatience, intolerance and other ego obstructions.

(vii) An important resolution required for a person who is attempting personal growth is that one should *believe in ones own development and ability* to relinquish the negative habits that have been holding one back.

Also, from time to time it is good to assess or take stock of oneself — how one is going, how one is thinking, and to feel good about one's achievements, involvements or contribution. The structure and nature of human beings is such that all, without exception, have a divine spark and are capable of expressing goodness.

# CHAPTER 10

# Psychophysiological Practices

1. Mental Quietening

2. Listening

3. Equal Breathing

4. Replacement of Ideas

5. Contemplating Your Place in the Universe

FOR the health of the body and mind a very consistent and almost regimented routine is required. This must become part of one's way of living that is practised every day without fail.

There are a number of psychophysiological practices available, collectively termed the Yogendra System*,

*The Yogendra System of Healthy Living is an integrated system of stress management, musculo-skeletal strengthening and personal development. Using gentle psychophysical practices, simple but effective breathing routines and mental quietening techniques, the individual is taught how to improve vitality, develop concentration, increase resilience and manage stress more effectively. The program, which is initially run over six weeks, has no particular religious framework and readily accomodates individuals' personal philosophies and beliefs. These practices are based on traditional techniques which my father taught and modified to suit contemporary individuals. I have further modified them to suit the psychology of the contemporary western individual.

which cater for the needs of the physical body, the spine, nervous system, circulatory system, digestive system and respiratory system. There are also semi-meditative techniques that regenerate and quieten the mind to facilitate gaining peace and tranquillity.

When we practise techniques that address the needs of the "body-mind complex" in a comprehensive manner, we find that we are more cheerful, more peaceful, and more at ease in life. Our overall approach, efficiency and contribution in any sphere improves. This gives self-confidence, increases self-esteem, and gives us a sense of positive self-worth.

The techniques described below are practical approaches and should be practiced daily. The sequence of the routine, the duration of practice and other details are discussed later.

## 1. Mental Quietening

This technique enables you to develop a sense of concentration, a feeling of control over the mind, of the object of its focus, and a sense of abstraction and standing back from incoming and outgoing thoughts.

Because the mind is full of ideas, associations and distractions, it will be difficult in the initial stages to control the activities of the mind, to enable it to become quieter and more peaceful. It is therefore important that in order to achieve a state of quietude, you attempt the practice with a very definite attitude.

Today we find that people are talking more and more about meditation and numerous techniques are being recommended. People involve themselves in visualisation, colours or breathing, and listening to music that is gentle and peaceful. If you want to learn meditation as it is understood in a more fundamental sense, then it will be better to start with something more simple. Although it may seem to be less inter-esting, it will take you further.

You first need to find and adopt a posture that is comfortable and have a fixed time and duration in which you attempt this practice every day as part of your routine.

Once a position which is comfortable (e.g. sitting reasonably straight in a chair or cross legged with the support of a cushion or blanket) is taken up, you must practice to the point where you can hold this position for 20 to 30 minutes without any interruptions from the body-mind complex. When you can sustain this, you begin the practice by trying to centralise your attention and dissociate from thoughts and emotions. Attempt to get into the mode of observation, of being a witness or observer.

It is like, for example, if you were driving down a highway, stopped, got out of the car, and stood back on the kerbside: other cars keep going by, like thoughts passing through the mind, and you just watch them, standing back observing.

When observing yourself, you can also notice the breathing and the rate of breathing. As you become more aware of the breathing do not interfere with it but attempt to gently synchronise your thinking with the breathing, following along as the breath comes in or goes out. Thus you begins to establish a rhythm which begins to settle the thought processes.

Sometimes, when you manage to allow this to happen, you begin to feel more composed and much clearer. You can then try to go deeper, as if withdrawing from the outside world and going further within yourself. As you do this, simply aim to hold there.

This mental quietening practice should be developed to the point where one is able to do it for around 30 minutes.

## 2. Listening

The posture to take up for this technique is sitting against a wall with your legs outstretched in front and hands in your lap. This practice is difficult to start with and thus it is recommended that you initially start listening to the sounds in the external environment first. Sounds that are continuous, sounds that are not interrupted too often are best. You pick one that is more pronounced. Listen to that as long as possible, and if it disappears or fades away, then pick up the next sound. In this manner you can develop the attitude of listening to a sound for a prolonged period. This should be continued for a period of 10 to 15 minutes.

When you have done this practice for two or three months or more, then you can begin to go within and listen more inwardly to whatever is there. As you turn more inwardly, you may experience a sense of silence. When you do, you can begin listening to any sounds occurring within yourself; perhaps you may become aware of your heartbeat or a pulsation or a vibration in the body. As such, you become interested and conscious of this rhythm and allow yourself to continuously remain attuned to and involved in this internal sound. This should be continued for around 20 minutes.

This practice is very meaningful and those individuals who have learned it and been doing it for many years, find that they are far more relaxed, mentally quieter and clearer, almost non-aggressive, and have built up a stronger sense of self-esteem.

One should not take this technique lightly. Only consistent practice over time will yield the result you anticipate. The minimum time for this practice to be meaningful to any individual is from four to six months after which, if the practice is done well, along with other approaches, one can find oneself with a much stronger sense of mental clarity and strength than when one started.

## 3. Equal Breathing

Initially, take a standing posture with your feet about eight to nine inches apart, toes slightly inward to make the feet parallel, and stand as straight as you can with arms by your side, resting and relaxed.

Start inhaling slowly and consciously, not trying to fill up the lungs with one massive breath, but allowing the breath to come gently, observing the breath coming into the nostrils, trying to allow it to filter through the epiglottal region in the neck and filling the lungs from the bottom upwards. Take the breath in as long and as comfortably as you can, and note the time you took taking the breath in. Then reverse the cycle and breath out, again very gently in a steady and controlled way, and time yourself.

You then note that you are breathing in for anywhere between three seconds to fifteen seconds, and breathing out for four seconds to sixteen seconds. The rate varies between individuals and there are no standards other than the one you establish for yourself and which are comfortable for you.

Out of your own experience, select the standard that is convenient and comfortable to you.

For example, if a person has taken seven seconds in and has been able to breathe out eight or nine seconds, then that person should attempt to only breath in for five seconds — even though they may have the capacity to go further — and also breath out for five seconds — even though they may also have the capacity to breathe out further. Therefore the five seconds in and five seconds out will become the equal breathing rate for that person. Those with twelve and fifteen seconds may drop to ten seconds in and ten seconds out. Thus, you determine your equal breathing rate by reducing the count from the practice breathing round, to a slightly lower count which is more comfortable for you and equal in duration for the inward and outward breath. It should be comfortable enough so that you can sustain this rate for fifteen rounds (one round is an inward and outward breath).

In the initial stages while you are getting used to this technique, you might do five rounds in and out in an equal fashion and then pause. Then do another five rounds with a break, and a final five rounds to make a total of fifteen rounds. Once you become habituated to this for a period of a month or so, you can then start doing it straight for fifteen times.

Some people feel light-headed or dizzy when they first attempt this type of breathing technique but this is only a temporary effect of hyperventilation which disappears with continued practice. Should your attempt give you an adverse reaction, then our recommendation is to discontinue it totally until you can seek some further advice.

It is also important to emphasise that the aim of the equal breathing technique is not to increase the length of each breath to make them longer and longer, but more to focus on the smoothness and consistency of each breath; to make the inward breath the same as the outward breath.

## 4. Replacement of Ideas

Quite often you are caught up in an almost obsessive way with an idea or a thought process that you find very hard to get rid of. It continuously niggles at you and becomes stuck in your mind. At such times, if you have already practised and trained yourself, you could overcome it.

This technique prepares you and strengthens your mind so that you eventually can overcome repetitive negative thoughts and themes.

The practice consists of, from time to time in the day, catching yourself thinking and interrupting the particular train of thought process going on. You deliberately distract yourself at that moment, and switch tracks towards something which, preferably, has a more mathematical or calculative element. For example, you actually count the petals of a flower or leaves in a tree, or tiles or bricks — or whatever is around you. You can count this from one to one hundred, or perhaps more. As you practise, you become so involved in this process of distracting yourself with counting that you are able to break the cycle that has been nagging you. You should perform this practice six or seven times each day for approximately five to ten minutes.

Sometimes, in the early stages, the negative thought may return after you have done this practice. It has nevertheless been weakened and will become progressively easier to control over time. Over a period of time you get into a habit that enables you to distract yourself and get away from the obsessive, irritating, repetitive thoughts.

## 5. Contemplating Your Place in the Universe

This technique involves reflecting on and trying to understand your place in the universe.

We know it has been said and experienced by many who are wise souls that there is a state of being where everything that is outside us, spreading right through the universe, is available to us within ourselves. Further, there is an aspect of what is available within us of this expanse of phenomena which goes further and further towards eternity.

It is interesting to think about the relative dimensions of phenomena in the world: the smallness of things and the enormity of other things. In this technique, you seek to find your place in all of this, to locate yourself somewhere within this vast scale of things and reflect on the fact that in the entire universe,

"I am important as well as unimportant". Why do I bother so often to feel that I have to be always important, or alternatively, remain always unimportant? Can I not be in between where I feel happy doing what I have to do rather than feel I have to know my importance or lack of importance? Can I not be content just to participate in things without referring everything back to this sense of presumed importance?

Quite often when you work this through in your mind repeatedly, placing yourself in a position where you feel that you really belong in this whole phenomena of life, the pressures of other people's thinking seem to vanish and you are able to establish more securely your own identity and belief in yourself.

These are some of the techniques that can be incorporated into your everyday routine. Wherever there is any misunderstanding or uncertainty, it is wiser not to attempt a technique until you are clear about what you are doing.

The ideal daily sequence for these techniques is to begin, first thing in the morning, with *Equal Breathing* and then the *Mental Quietening*. If you have time, you can also do the *Listening* practice. The *Listening* and *Contemplating Your Place* practices can be done in the evening or any time during the day. *Replacement of Thoughts* should be done at appropriate intervals during each day.

# CHAPTER 11
# The Art of Being

THERE IS a tremendous amount of beauty in "just being" — where you have withdrawn from automatically reacting, responding to, and suffering other's reactions. You hold yourself together — all impatience, emotional reactions, and associated thought processes are held quiet in your own being — and you do not allow these to disturb your thinking patterns, nor make you react to precipitate an approach, attitude or action which compounds the situation.

The idea of "just being", from time to time in a day, is a beautiful way of being relaxed, of being free from stress or anxiety. All the composite factors within you are resting and you are "just being".

In the world as we see it, it is the responses and reactions we suffer that become the factors that motivate and precipitate our conscious actions and reactions. This ultimately allows life to progress, and from that amalgam there develops a search, an urge to find our own selves. The subconscious becomes organised at a deeper level to search for a meaning from all of the reactions and responses that we are enduring. It tries to throw them up to the conscious level, where we can discern and know more about our being.

Furthermore, we see that when we have a response to any stimulus, to that response there is another response, a secondary reaction within us to our initial reaction. Of course, at times there may be just one response without any flow-on reaction to the initial reaction, but the majority of times we do get caught up in the process of reacting to our responses all over again.

Therefore you have to have a very strong approach to your thinking, to the point that this right thinking, or disciplining of the mind, will allow you to overcome, control, or hold together your mind when you have reacted. If you cannot do this, it is like spending money on something, and then having to spend again on the very same thing — obviously it is a waste. In the same way it is a waste of your mind or mental energy to be thinking again, responding again, when you already have had that experience of reacting.

Often when we have responded to a situation, through our imagination and memories of previous experiences, we seem to re-enact the dialogue and relive the drama, and go over again the whole episode in our minds.

Instead of being so reactive, you should allow yourself to settle down from anything that has created a reaction, a response, or that has traumatised you. The more effective approach is to sit back and wait, to think it through, and not create a new response sequence out of that which you have reacted to. Take what has happened step by step, dissect it step by step, look to the cause of the response or reaction occurring within you. Then assess what it was that happened, to which you reacted. If, to clarify your thinking, you have to write it down on paper, then it is better to do that to assist in thinking it through objectively.

There is no sense in any individual who has reacted, responded or become upset, to go again through the same process of upsetting him or herself. Rather it is better to sit back, look at it objectively, assess it and respond in a dignified way. Come to terms with the whole situation as if you are trying to find a method of rehabilitating the mind.

Practiced over time, this control or discipline allows you to focus the mind on finding the element of concentration. This state is where the mind is not fragmented, and you are able to control, concentrate and assess your reactions, come to a conclusion, and then refocus in such a way that your responses are appropriate and correct.

In your work situations, where unexpected things happen, go wrong, demands are made and decisions have to be taken, if you are able to control your reactions, the agitation of the mind, the fears and anxieties, even the euphoria of success, you can turn any situation into an asset by probing deeper into the whole system of reactions you had. If you can do this, then you add to your life, add to your vitality, and you add to your own being.

Because you cannot do the above, you find that you cannot be progressive, creative, or contribute in the highest way. Because, many times a day, you have reacted to the reactions and then reacted again, out of this has come your whole emotionalism, distortions and fears, which deprive you of the essential component of any successful approach, i.e. concentration. Since that depth of concentration is not available, you remain within the framework of what is easily possible and available, rather than "spreading your wings", and looking at new and creative frontiers. Distortions and confusion overtake your mind, and block its various faculties — particularly concentration and creativity — making them unavailable to you.

Consequently, there are difficulties within individuals, and groups, of coming to terms with themselves. Without the ability to remain focused on what is fundamental, life can become boring, dull, even threatening, since your motivations are not always positive. Your creative capacities are not responding, and the mind lacks the discipline to concentrate with this constant barrage of external and inner demands that come with the way that you are living.

On one hand, while you may have the need and urgency to achieve or find something deeper in life, the conscious mind, due to its lack of comprehension, cannot bring things together to give you the enthusiasm for life and satisfaction to make life palatable.

On the other hand, the subconscious mind feels or incorporates the pressure from the conscious mind and its pattern of thinking. The subconscious receives distorted, fragmented inputs mixed with varying degrees of impatience. This does not allow the individual to grow in a natural and happy way.

This is why it is very important that you keep yourself vibrantly healthy through maintaining a routine and regularly performing the quietening practices that you have learned, such as those described in this book. Give such practices a meaning and a status in your life. Conserve your vitality and those energies, sexual or otherwise, which give the nervous system the stability and the strength to face up to and overcome the demands that are made all the time on you by the society, your family, co-workers, and others.

Slowly, through this approach, you will control your conscious and subconscious processes, and the impressions of the inner and external world that come within your comprehension will be well organised, and will work well for you.

Our future is always created by the impressions we have accumulated in the subconscious in the past, as well as those impressions that we are now involved with in the present. The future is a continuation of the amalgamation of our past actions and reactions. But we really must learn to recognise and accept that we only live in the present moment as we go through life. The eternal is now, and now is the only aware-ness we really have. If we are seeking happiness and understanding, then we must try to live in the present, in a more "internalised state of being".

It is good to have these ideas going through your minds to grapple with, to try to understand, to refine them, and to find meaning and strength from them. Although we have, to varying degrees, educated our conscious mind, we have never tried to educate the subconscious mind to any degree — other than what happens accidentally or, rarely, through the impact of controlling aspects of the conscious mind.

It is a wonderful feeling to realise that there is no time in the past or the future, that there is only one eternal now. It holds the quality of all that the mind contains. Worries and anxieties about the future, or concerns from the past are a very confused way of relating to life and are linked to the subconscious state. This subconscious state is fraught with un-reasonable doubts and fears that combine with the imagination, and often distort our perception and men-tal images. Sometimes this occurs to the extent of causing the conscious mind to become paralysed and non-functional.

While the subconscious mind wants to clean up its domain and move along with knowing and progressing, the conscious mind, aided and assisted by the ego, holds up the progress of the subconscious. This results in negative thinking suffused with fears, worries and doubts, and takes away any faith in oneself. This is ultimately due to a lack of understanding of how the mind works.

Quite often it is the case that the conscious never lets the subconscious rest, nor does the subconscious allow the conscious to rest. There are always demands and counter-demands that go on. This is a process of inner conflict that has to be restricted, contained and overcome. Ideally, all we should have to determine is that the external and internal demands are basically reasonable, that they are appropriate, creative and constructive. How often do we come to a crossroad, where on one side we say "I'd like to do this", and another part of us says "I don't know if I can"? It is impossible for anyone to handle two opposing thoughts at the same time. A solution is required for us to proceed.

These are the types of confusions that we allow within ourselves, creating the dualities and the doubts that we live with. Therefore to live a more purposeful life one must be far more definitive in what one wants, needs and seeks to achieve. The ambivalence with which we live — "maybe, or maybe not", "could be, or could be not" — is never helpful in building our confidence, self-esteem and self-worth. To progress we need to resolve the obstacles of our inner oppositions and conflicts.

In fact the only way you can keep yourself free from the conflicting thoughts, is by controlling the process of thinking itself. This will be perhaps the most important move you will ever make, if you are not already on the way to making it.

Our worries and concerns are a state of mind that we suffer because of the ambivalence and conflict. It is not necessary for you to remain confused all the time, for all of your life. To be free from such concerns will assist you in gaining greater power and control over your subconscious mind.

In your subconscious there are thoughts that you have suppressed, that are hiding there, wanting to be vented and to be expressed — ready to spring out at a moments notice. If these thoughts are allowed to proceed freely through to the conscious mind, then they can consume all the power of the mind, erode your confidence and cause you additional confusion.

So it is important that you develop an ability to understand your personal thinking processes, and to assess what should be eliminated, rather than giving credence or importance to anything and everything that comes to the surface from the subconscious. The only way you can get yourself into a position of strength is by recognising that you must allow, in a systematic and controlled way, all the thoughts you have to be fully accepted, looked at, assessed, properly thought through, and eventually disposed or acted upon as you see fit.

To assist in this process, try to do the following. Every day you must try to concentrate on refining your individual awareness through practising the techniques described in the previous chapter. More particularly, you should practice "just being". Sit down and allow your awareness to free itself from the thoughts, ideas, fears, and anxieties — and be silent. Hold this awareness for as long as you can, keep bringing yourself back whenever you stray from it, until you are able to be free of thoughts and remain totally aware. You will then start understanding the process better, and begin to control the mind more effectively.

Even though your past attempts may not have helped you achieve much, or have frustrated you, you must endeavour to renew your efforts. Only through repeated practice will you attain progress and achieve a really worthwhile state of "being".

# CHAPTER 11

# Conclusion

IF THESE REMARKS make sense to you, and provoke your conscience, then you have to start on yourself to find out how much love you have to give and share, how much love you need to feel safe and secure, the expectations you are labouring under and putting on others. As well, how much guilt have you accumulated, and how much guilt have you brought about in others? How much stress are you feeling and how much stress are you causing? These are the issues that every individual will have to confront and work on.

Life is a process of education, a process of understanding and finding a deeper meaning and greater purpose for our existence. One has to make every attempt to broaden one's outlook, understanding the fundamental issues, and seeking guidance on how to progress towards a healthier and happier life.

There is a great experience awaiting you which becomes available when you find your own "uniqueness". Your uniqueness is that pure quality exhibited by your true self. The solution to all your problems ultimately resides in expressing this quality in your everyday living. It is where you will find true growth. It is what will give you real contentment of being and

joy in your heart. Do not let anyone break your resolve to grow and find yourself. And remember, your
life patterns change people around you; by changing
yourself you change the world.